D0841155

the transcendence of the ego

the transcendence of the ego

AN EXISTENTIALIST THEORY OF CONSCIOUSNESS

by Jean-Paul Sartre

TRANSLATED AND ANNOTATED
WITH AN INTRODUCTION BY
Forrest Williams and Robert Kirkpatrick

THE NOONDAY PRESS
A DIVISION OF
FARRAR, STRAUS AND GIROUX   NEW YORK

contents

acknowledgments

The present work is a translation of "La Transcendance de L'Ego: Esquisse d'une description phénoménologique." The original French version appeared in *Recherches Philosophiques*, VI, 1936-37.

The author and the copyright owners, Librairie A. Hatier, 8 Rue d'Assas, Paris, France, have kindly given their permission for the present translation. For financial assistance provided by the Council on Research and Creative Work of the University of Colorado, the translators make grateful acknowlededgment.

translators' introduction

La Transcendance de l'Ego, although a comparatively short work, may fairly be regarded as a turning-point in the philosophical development of Jean-Paul Sartre, the leader of French existentialism. Prior to the writing of this essay, published in 1937, Sartre had been intimately acquainted with the phenomenological movement which originated in Germany with Edmund Husserl. It is a fundamental tenet of the phenomenology of Husserl which is here attacked by

Sartre. We should like to indicate briefly what is under attack by referring to the philosophy of Husserl, and to suggest how this disagreement with Husserl seems to have facilitated the transition from phenomenology to the existentialist doctrines of *L'Etre et le Néant*.[1]

The phenomenology of Husserl was a reflexive inquiry, or a philosophy of consciousness. The name "phenomenology," indeed, means the "logos of phenomena," that is to say, the truth or rationale of immediate experience. Thus characterized, however, the phenomenology of Husserl would be difficult to distinguish from Kantian epistemology, which was also a philosophy of consciousness—more exactly, an account of the principles of the mind presupposed by science and mathematics. Naturally, in phenomenology everything turns on what one understands by "consciousness," which designates the subject matter of investigation. The particular attraction of phenomenology to its many disciples in Germany and elsewhere seems to have been the emphasis on the "intentionality" of consciousness.

[1] Paris: Gallimard, 1943. An English translation by Hazel E. Barnes has been published under the title *Being and Nothingness* (New York: Philosophical Library, 1956).

Consciousness, Husserl stressed, is consciousness *of* an object, and composes no part of the object. Consequently, even if necessary laws of the activity of consciousness can be established, as in the philosophy of Kant, such laws would never add up to an account of the essential character of any object of consciousness.

At first thought, this contention may seem to be a truism. For example, consciousness and planets obviously have their own respective natures, constituting topics for investigation quite distinct from each other. But Kant and others have in some sense maintained the contrary even with regard to the knowable movements of the planets. In doing so they have sometimes distinguished between the empirical laws of the mind and its non-empirical or "a priori" principles. But the net effect is always a partial or total reduction of questions concerning the nature of objects to questions concerning the nature of the activity of thought. This tactic may seem especially plausible with respect to, say, numbers or chimeras. Is not the arithmetical formula "$2 + 2 = 4$," or the lion-headed serpent of my dream, in a rather obvious sense a mental event? And therefore should not an epistemological account of the nature of numbers or of imaginary things be a study of the mental activity of counting or feigning? To the phenomenologist, such leading questions betray serious confusion through failure to recognize the subtleties in the notion of "mental" introduced by the intentionality of consciousness.

If by "mental" one means that the thing so called does not exist anywhere in space, then of course an arithmetical formula or a chimera is mental. But if by "mental" one further means that the thing so called exists as a mental activity, viz., consists in the act of calculating or the act of imagining, then arithmetical formulas and chimeras are certainly *not* "mental." For the formula and the chimerical monster are the *intended objects* of the mental activities of calculating and imagining. The mental act of addition is not the numerical sum; the mental act of feigning a monster is not the feigned monster; the mental act of judging is not the state of affairs judged to be the case; the mental act of enjoyment is not the value enjoyed; and, in general, consciousness always acts so as to intend an object or objects *standing over against its activity*.

To many philosophers, including Sartre, the refreshing consequence of the phenomenology of Husserl was that intentional objects of every sort, existent and non-existent, can and should be described in their own right. Theory of knowledge need not be closeted with the activities of consciousness, but could go directly in reflection to the intended objects of consciousness and the principles governing *them*. Thus, number theory (to which Husserl early made some interesting contributions) would not be concerned with certain mental syntheses, as in Kant or Mill, but with numbers themselves, their intrinsic character and their relations, as intentional objects of consciousness. Similarly, aesthetics would not reduce itself to a study of taste, but would study aesthetic objects and their principles. Likewise, intended moral values need not be treated indirectly in terms of the principles of choice. For consciousness is always turned outward by its own activity, looking at or judging an object or state of affairs which is not the looking or judging; and at any level of reflection, in which the activity of consciousness turns upon itself, an intended object remains visible, distinct from any act of awareness.

Naturally, reflexive examination of intentional objects must forego any attempt to establish what does and does not in fact exist. It is, rather, an attempt to discern the principles governing different types of intentional objects. Logically speaking, such phenomenological inquiry is presupposed by science, mathematics, moral controversy, etc., since one must make the general distinctions between existence, illusion, numbers, moral ideals, and so forth, in order to institute relevant methods of inquiry. For example, to determine whether other planets than our own exist, one must have some idea of what it is to exist as a physical body. Along similar lines, among psychologists there is unceasing disagreement concerning the distinction, if there be any, between "physical" and "psychical" events. The viewpoint of both Husserl and Sartre is that such confusions arise from a failure to base fundamental concepts and particular methods of empirical investigation upon prior phenomenological inquiry.

In order to make certain, however, that phenomenological study of the principles of objects would not illicitly become a magical substitute for the hardships of empirical investigation, Husserl insisted that the phenomenologist "bracket" questions of fact. By such "reduction" or "epoché," as this precaution is called, the phenomenologist discounts in reflection all evidence for one's own existence as a particular person. Thus, he studies consciousness intending objects, not as an event happening to a certain person in the world, but as a pure phenomenon—*"ein Schauspiel nur."*

With the phenomenological program as described, Sartre remained essentially in agreement in the following essay. Like Husserl, Sartre seems to have been particularly concerned with mapping out different types of intentional objects, e.g., the physical body, number, value, the psyche, the psycho-physical person. Like Husserl, Sartre anticipated consequences for the methodology of the sciences of man. (To cite a specific instance, Sartre, like Husserl, regarded the Freudian notion of "unconscious thought" as either a contradiction or a grotesque misnomer.) All the disagreement between Sartre and Husserl centers in this essay on a single question: whether consciousness can be found after a "reduction" to be presided over by a "transcendental ego," that is to say, an "I" or subject essentially involved no less than objects in the very possibility of any act of consciousness whatsoever. The ego affirmed by Husserl and denied by Sartre is not, of course, the existing person, for, as we have already seen, all evidence bearing on what does or does not exist in nature and human society is discounted by Husserl.

Sartre's denial of a transcendental ego might be considered nothing more than a family quarrel within phenomenology. But there are two very good reasons why this dispute with Husserl cannot be regarded as a trivial disagreement over a minor item of phenomenological doctrine. First, the affirmation of a transcendental ego seems to do nothing less than reverse the initial claim of phenomenology to be able to investigate objects in their own right. Instead, it renders objects dependent for their various characteristics upon the activity of the ego. As can readily be imagined, to many disciples of Husserl (and to Sartre as well, as the present essay clearly indicates), such a turn of events in phenomenology constituted a betrayal by Husserl of what was most fruitful in the phenomenologist's emphasis upon the intentionality of consciousness. Second, by denying a transcendental ego and reinstating the object of consciousness in its primacy —or "intentionality" in its original significance for Husserlian phenomenology—Sartre stirred to life the entire complex of problems later pursued by his own brand of existential philosophy. If we look briefly at these two matters in turn, we can, in retrospect, see the present essay as a turning-point in the thought of Sartre, a transition from Husserlian phenomenology to the full-blown existentialism of *L'Etre et le Néant*.

Let us suppose, as Husserl claimed, that a transcendental ego "stands behind" consciousness. If such an ego-endowed consciousness is, as Husserl also maintained, an intentional consciousness, then the ego must make contact with some reality different from itself. Otherwise, of course, the ego is simply caught up in the circle of its own subjectivity. The epistemological problem, therefore, is to understand how such contact is possible. Clearly, an intermediary or third reality will be needed which (on pain of infinite regress) will have to combine characteristics of both the ego and its objects. There results the notion of a hybrid stuff (termed *hylé* by Husserl) which is "contained in" consciousness but is able to "represent" or "resemble" the objects intended by the ego. In perception, for example, a transcendental ego "stands behind" the various intentional activities of consciousness. Thus, what we directly perceive (e.g., the colored shape I see) will be interpreted as material for the intentional activity of the ego, rather than as an object having a character in its own right— as the potter's clay rather than the pot. The intentional *object*, in turn, will be considered a product of the activity of the transcendental ego upon such directly given contents of consciousness, usually called "sense data." And the true study of the intentional object in phenomenology—contrary to the original tendency of Husserl's philosophy—will be a study of the principles governing the activity of the transcendental ego by which the object is constituted out of such contents. In sum, a phenomenology that admits a transcendental ego standing behind the acts of consciousness must also discover that consciousness has contents and must end by referring the character of every object to the activity of consciousness. To many disciples of Husserl, this outcome of phenomenology was simply another version of the philosophy of Kant, notwithstanding the initial tendency of phenomenology in a seemingly new direction.

Such ironic consequences need not be suffered by the phenomenologist, however, *if* Husserl is mistaken concerning the transcendental ego.

Hence, Sartre goes to the heart of the matter in the following essay. His contention is precisely that there is no ego "in" or "behind" consciousness. There is only an ego *for* consciousness. The ego is "out there," in the world, an object among objects. The question may now be asked: by whom or by what shall the *contents* of consciousness be fashioned into intended objects for consciousness, since this duty was performed in the phenomenology of Husserl by the transcendental ego? And the answer given by Sartre is that nothing shall constitute contents of consciousness into intended objects, for the important reason that *consciousness has no contents*. All content is on the side of the object. Consciousness contains neither transcendental ego nor anything else. It is simply a spontaneity, a sheer activity transcending toward objects. There are no mental entities whatsoever, no "whats" which are of the "stuff" of consciousness, but function as representatives of the outside world. Thus, all so-called "images," "representations," "ideas," "phenomena," "sense data," etc., are objects *for* consciousness, not contents *in* consciousness. Like William James, Sartre insists that representational theories of knowledge violate our sense of life. When we see a mountain, or imagine one, it is a mountain we are seeing or imagining, not our idea of a mountain. Consciousness is present to objects. To use the metaphorical language sometimes employed by Sartre (since literal usage tends to suggest objects rather than consciousness), consciousness is a great emptiness, a wind blowing toward objects. Its whole reality is exhausted in intending what is other. It is never "self-contained," or container; it is always "outside itself." Thus, whereas for Husserl intentionality is *one* essential feature of any consciousness, for Sartre intentionality *is* consciousness. On this view, the character of the object of consciousness regains its independence for phenomenological investigation and becomes analyzable in its own right (as in the original phenomenological theory of intentionality).

If we turn to *L'Etre et le Néant*, we find that Sartre adheres in that later work to all the consequences of his earlier emphasis on the notion of the intentionality of consciousness. Indeed, almost the entire novelty of Sartre's major work consists in the radical distinction between consciousness and absolutely everything else, that is, between intentionality and the non-intentional.

Sartre insists that these are two different types of being. And the key terms of *L'Etre et le Néant*, *pour-soi* and *en-soi*, or the "for-itself" and the "in-itself," are merely alternative terms for this distinction within being. The major part of that work consists of skillful phenomenological descriptions of the various ways in which these totally distinct types of being function in human experience.

Moreover, the rejection of the transcendental ego and the return to the phenomenological doctrine of intentionality in its original significance had a radical consequence—seemingly not fully evident to Sartre himself at the time of the following essay—which led directly to existentialism, that is, to a philosophy of human existence. The radical consequence is that the important Husserlian technique of "reduction" or "epoché" is impossible. For, if consciousness has no transcendental ego and no contents whatsoever, such suspension of all affirmations of existence beyond consciousness itself must be construed as reflection upon intentions of consciousness which no longer posit any objects in an existing world. But if the being of objects, or being "in-itself," is not constructed by a transcendental ego out of contents of consciousness, as Husserl claimed, then the being of objects either is discovered to every act of consciousness, or can never be found by any act of consciousness. The latter alternative denies that we can ever apprehend anything having a type of being different from the being of consciousness, and thus denies the principle of the intentionality of consciousness which Sartre upholds without reservation.

Consequently, after his essay on the ego, Sartre must acknowledge that the being of objects, or being "in-itself," is discovered *without exception* to every act of consciousness. In other words, consciousness must be for Sartre nothing but a "revealing intuition" of things, the being of which is everywhere. There can be no exceptional act of consciousness, therefore, by which the phenomenologist has the privilege of suspending in reflection all affirmations of existence regarding objects in order to contemplate the being of consciousness alone. Consciousness, rather, is never alone, is never isolated from the existing world. Not only is the Husserlian technique of reduction unthinkable within the framework of Sartre's essay on the ego, but if accomplished (*per impossible*) such reduction would not make possible a reflexive investigation of anything at all, not even consciousness. For such "reduction" would be a contraction of intentional consciousness into itself: a kind of Brahmanic annihilation of consciousness.

The radical consequence for Sartre, fully manifest in *L'Etre et le Néant*, is that there can be no reflexive or phenomenological philosophy occupied with a consciousness shut off or separable from the world, even as a fiction for specified analytical purposes. Involvement in the existing world, which Husserl invidiously termed "the natural standpoint" in contrast to the "reduced, neutral standpoint" of his philosophy, must be quite inescapable for consciousness, and therefore inescapable for phenomenology itself.

Thus, with no transcendental ego or contents to clutter up consciousness, phenomenology, or the reflexive study of consciousness, becomes directly occupied with human existence in its concrete relations to the world, with the nature of man as a consciousness of things, of himself, and of other selves. It is precisely such a phenomenological description of human existence in its "situation-in-the-world"—"phenomenological ontology. as the subtitle of *L'Etre et le Néant* proclaims—that constitutes the goal of Sartre's existentialism, as contrasted to the more logical and abstract purposes of Husserlian phenomenology.

The existentialist orientation is thus toward concrete human dilemmas, toward human emotion and human conflict, rather than toward science and mathematics. But this is in the first instance an orientation already freed, by the following essay, from the notion of a transcendental ego and the many associated issues. Perhaps, indeed, it was largely because Husserl found the problems surrounding his doctrine of the transcendental ego so complex that the problems of man as he exists remained always out of his grasp as a phenomenologist.

But Sartre's reorientation of phenomenology toward a consciousness necessarily present to the existing world, although facilitated by the essay rejecting the transcendental ego, is not without its own special problems. Being, Sartre had recognized, is everywhere. Since every act of consciousness reveals being, the crucial phenomenological problem now becomes that of explaining, as in *The Sophist*, our encounters with otherness and negation in the world. In short, *non*-being is the philosophical challenge. A detailed phenomenological investigation of being and nothingness, and of man as their ontologically tortured expression, becomes the task of philosophy. It is to this task that Sartre devotes himself, a decade after the following essay, in *L'Etre et le Néant*.

ROBERT KIRKPATRICK
University of Utah

FORREST WILLIAMS
University of Colorado

the transcendence of the ego

For most philosophers the ego is an "inhabitant" of consciousness. Some affirm its formal presence at the heart of *Erlebnisse*, as an empty principle of unification. Others—psychologists for the most part—claim to discover its material presence, as the center of desires and acts, in each moment of our psychic life. We should like to show here that the ego is neither formally nor materially *in* consciousness: it is outside, *in the world*. It is a being of the world, like the ego of another.

i the I and the Me

A. THE THEORY OF THE FORMAL PRESENCE OF THE *I*

It must be conceded to Kant that "the I Think *must be able* to accompany all our representations." But need we then conclude that an *I in fact* inhabits all our states of consciousness and actually effects the supreme synthesis of our experience? This inference would appear to distort the Kantian view. The Critical problem being one of validity, Kant says nothing concerning the actual existence of the *I Think*. On the contrary, he seems to have seen perfectly well that there are moments of consciousness without the *I*, for he says "*must be able* to accompany." The problem, indeed, is to determine the conditions for the possibility of experience. One of these conditions is that I can always regard my perception or thought as *mine:* nothing more. But there is in contemporary philosophy a dangerous tendency —traces of which may be found in neo-Kantianism, empirico-Criticism, and an intellectualism like that of Brochard—which consists of making into a reality the conditions, determined by Criti-

cism, for the possibility of experience. This is the
tendency which leads certain writers to ask, for
example, what "transcendental consciousness"
can *be*. If one poses the problem in these terms,
one is naturally constrained to conceive this consciousness—which is constitutive of our empirical
consciousness—as an unconscious. But Boutroux,
in his lectures on the philosophy of Kant, has already dealt sufficiently with these interpreta-
tions. The preoccupation of Kant was never with
the way in which empirical consciousness is *in
fact* constituted. He never deduced empirical
consciousness, in the manner of a Neo-Platonic
process, from a higher consciousness, from a constituting hyper-consciousness. For Kant, transcendental consciousness is nothing but the set of
conditions which are necessary for the existence
of an empirical consciousness. Consequently, *to
make into a reality* the transcendental *I*, to make
of it the inseparable companion of each of our
"consciousnesses," [1] is to pass on *fact*, not on
validity, and to take a point of view radically
different from that of Kant. And then to cite as
justification Kantian considerations on the unity
necessary to experience would be to commit the
very error of those who make transcendental
consciousness into a pre-empirical unconscious.

If we associate with Kant, therefore, the question of validity, the question of fact is still not broached. Consequently, it may be posed succinctly at this point: the *I think* must be able to accompany all our representations, but does it in fact accompany them? Supposing, moreover, that a certain representation, A, passes from some state unaccompanied by the *I Think* to a state in which the *I Think* does accompany it, will there follow a modification of the structure of A, or will the representation remain basically unchanged? This second question leads us to pose a third. The *I Think* must be able to accompany all our representations. But should we understand here that directly or indirectly the unity of our representations is effected by the *I Think*, or that the representations of a consciousness must be united and articulated in such a way that it is always possible in their regard to note an *I Think?* This third question seems to arise at the level of validity and, at this level, seems to renounce Kantian orthodoxy. But it is actually a question of fact, which may be formulated thus: is the *I* that we encounter in our consciousness made possible by the synthetic unity of our representations, or is it the *I* which in fact unites the representations to each other?

If we reject all the more or less forced interpre-
tations of the *I Think* offered by the post-Kant-
ians, and nevertheless wish to solve the problem
of the existence *in fact* of the *I* in consciousness,
we meet on our path the phenomenology of Husserl. Phenomenology is a scientific, not a Critical,
study of consciousness. Its essential way of pro-
ceeding is by intuition.[2] Intuition, according to
Husserl, puts us in the presence of *the thing*. We
must recognize, therefore, that phenomenology
is a science of *fact*, and that the problems it poses
are problems *of fact*;[3] which can be seen, moreover, from Husserl's designation of phenomenology as a *descriptive* science. Problems concerning the relations of the *I* to consciousness are
therefore existential problems. Husserl, too, dis-
covers the transcendental consciousness of Kant,
and grasps it by the ἐποχή.[4] But this consciousness is no longer a set of logical conditions. It is a
fact which is absolute. Nor is this transcendental
consciousness a hypostatization of validity, an
unconscious which floats between the real and
the ideal. It is a real consciousness accessible to
each of us as soon as the "reduction" is performed. And it is indeed this transcendental
consciousness which constitutes our empirical
consciousness, our consciousness "in the world,"

our consciousness with its psychic and psycho-physical *me*.

For our part, we readily acknowledge the existence of a constituting consciousness. We find admirable all of Husserl's descriptions in which he shows transcendental consciousness constituting the world by imprisoning itself in empirical consciousness. Like Husserl, we are persuaded that our psychic and psycho-physical *me* is a transcendent object which must fall before the ἐποχή. But we raise the following question: is not this psychic and psycho-physical *me* enough? Need one double it with a transcendental *I*, a structure of absolute consciousness?

The consequences of a reply are obvious. If the reply is negative, the consequences are:

First, the transcendental field becomes impersonal; or, if you like, "pre-personal," *without an I*.

Second, the *I* appears only at the level of humanity and is only one aspect of the *me*, the active aspect.

Third, the *I Think* can accompany our representations because it appears on a foundation of unity which it did not help to create; rather, this prior unity makes the *I Think* possible.

Fourth, one may well ask if personality (even

the abstract personality of an *I*) is a necessary accompaniment of a consciousness, and if one cannot conceive of absolutely impersonal consciousnesses.

To this question, Husserl has given his reply. After having determined (in *Logische Untersuchungen*[5]) that the *me* is a synthetic and transcendent production of consciousness, he reverted in *Ideen Zu Einer Reinen Phänomenologie Und Phänomenòlogischen Philosophie*[6] to the classic position of a transcendental *I*. This *I* would be, so to speak, behind each consciousness, a necessary structure of consciousnesses whose rays (*Ichstrahlen*) would light upon each phenomenon presenting itself in the field of attention. Thus transcendental consciousness becomes thoroughly personal. Was this notion necessary? Is it compatible with the definition of consciousness given by Husserl?[7]

It is ordinarily thought that the existence of a transcendental *I* may be justified by the need that consciousness has for unity and individuality. It is because all my perceptions and all my thoughts refer themselves back to this permanent seat that my consciousness is unified. It is because I can say *my* consciousness, and because Peter and Paul can also speak of *their* conscious-

nesses, that these consciousnesses distinguish
themselves from each other. The *I* is the producer of inwardness.

Now, it is certain that phenomenology does
not need to appeal to any such unifying and individualizing *I*. Indeed, consciousness is defined
by intentionality. By intentionality consciousness
transcends itself. It unifies itself by escaping
from itself. The unity of a thousand active consciousnesses by which I have added, do add,
and shall add two and two to make four, is the
transcendent object "two and two make four."
Without the permanence of this eternal truth a
real unity would be impossible to conceive, and
there would be irreducible operations as often as
there were operative consciousnesses. It is possible that those believing "two and two make four"
to be the *content* of my representation may be
obliged to appeal to a transcendental and subjective principle of unification, which will then
be the *I*. But it is precisely Husserl who has no
need of such a principle. The object is transcendent to the consciousnesses which grasp it, and it
is in the object that the unity of the consciousnesses is found.

It will be said that a principle of unity *within
duration* is nonetheless needed if the continual

flux of consciousness is to be capable of posit-
ing transcendent objects outside the flux. Consciousnesses must be perpetual syntheses of past
consciousnesses and present consciousness. This
is correct. But it is characteristic that Husserl,
who studied this subjective unification of consciousnesses in *Vorlesungen Zur Phänomenologie
Des Inneren Zeitbewusstseins*,[8] never had recourse to a synthetic power of the *I*. It is consciousness which unifies itself, concretely, by a
play of "transversal" intentionalities which are
concrete and real retentions of past consciousnesses. Thus consciousness refers perpetually to
itself. Whoever says "a consciousness" says "the
whole of consciousness," and this singular property belongs to consciousness itself, aside from
whatever relations it may have to the *I*. In
Cartesianische Meditationen,[9] Husserl seems to
have preserved intact this conception of consciousness unifying itself in time.

Furthermore, the individuality of consciousness evidently stems from the nature of consciousness. Consciousness (like Spinoza's substance) can be limited only by itself. Thus, it
constitutes a synthetic and individual totality en-
tirely isolated from other totalities of the same
type, and the *I* can evidently be only an *expres-*

sion (rather than a condition) of this incommunicability and inwardness of consciousnesses. Consequently we may reply without hesitation: the phenomenological conception of consciousness renders the unifying and individualizing role of the *I* totally useless. It is consciousness, on the contrary, which makes possible the unity and the personality of my *I*. The transcendental *I*, therefore, has no *raison d'être*.

But, in addition, this superfluous *I* would be a hindrance. If it existed it would tear consciousness from itself; it would divide consciousness; it would slide into every consciousness like an opaque blade. The transcendental *I* is the death of consciousness. Indeed, the existence of consciousness is an absolute because consciousness is consciousness of itself. This is to say that the type of existence of consciousness is to be consciousness of itself. And consciousness is aware of itself *in so far as it is consciousness of a transcendent object*. All is therefore clear and lucid in consciousness: the object with its characteristic opacity is before consciousness, but consciousness is purely and simply consciousness of being consciousness of that object. This is the law of its existence.

We should add that this consciousness of con-

sciousness—except in the case of reflective consciousness which we shall dwell on later—is not
positional, which is to say that consciousness is
not for itself its own object. Its object is by nature
outside of it, and that is why consciousness *posits*
and *grasps* the object in the same act. Consciousness knows itself only as absolute inwardness.
We shall call such a consciousness: consciousness in the first degree, or *unreflected* consciousness.

Now we ask: is there room for an *I* in such a
consciousness? The reply is clear: evidently not.
Indeed, such an *I* is not the object (since by
hypothesis the *I* is inner); nor is it an *I of consciousness*, since it is something for consciousness. It is not a translucent quality of consciousness, but would be in some way an inhabitant.
In fact, however formal, however abstract one
may suppose it to be, the *I*, with its personality,
would be a sort of center of opacity. It would be
to the concrete and psycho-physical *me* what a
point is to three dimensions: it would be an infinitely contracted *me*. Thus, if one introduces this
opacity into consciousness, one thereby destroys
the fruitful definition cited earlier. One congeals
consciousness, one darkens it. Consciousness is
then no longer a spontaneity; it bears within it-

self the germ of opaqueness. But in addition we
would be forced to abandon that original and
profound view which makes of consciousness a
non-substantial absolute. A pure consciousness
is an absolute quite simply because it is consciousness of itself. It remains therefore a "phenomenon" in the very special sense in which "to
be" and "to appear" are one. It is all lightness, all
translucence. This it is which differentiates the
Cogito of Husserl from the Cartesian *Cogito*. But
if the *I* were a necessary structure of consciousness, this opaque *I* would at once be raised to
the rank of an absolute. We would then be in the
presence of a monad. And this, indeed, is unfortunately the orientation of the new thought of
Husserl (see *Cartesianische Meditationen*[10]).
Consciousness is loaded down; consciousness has
lost that character which rendered it the absolute
existent *by virtue of non-existence*. It is heavy
and *ponderable*. All the results of phenomenology begin to crumble if the *I* is not, by the same
title as the world, a relative existent: that is to
say, an object *for* consciousness.

B. THE *cogito* AS REFLECTIVE CONSCIOUSNESS

The Kantian *I Think* is a condition of possibility.
The *Cogito* of Descartes and of Husserl is an apprehension of fact. We have heard of the "factual necessity" [11] of the *Cogito*, and this phrase
seems to me most apt. Also, it is undeniable that
the *Cogito* is personal. In the *I Think* there is an
I who thinks. We attain here the *I* in its purity,
and it is indeed from the *Cogito* that an "Egology" must take its point of departure. The fact
that can serve for a start is, then, this one: each
time we apprehend our thought, whether by an
immediate intuition or by an intuition based on
memory, we apprehend an *I* which is the *I* of the
apprehended thought, and which is given, in addition, as transcending this thought and all other
possible thoughts. If, for example, I want to remember a certain landscape perceived yesterday
from the train, it is possible for me to bring back
the memory of that landscape as such. But I can
also recollect that *I* was seeing that landscape.
This is what Husserl calls, in *Vorlesungen Zur
Phänomenologie Des Inneren Zeitbewusstseins*,[12]
the possibility of *reflecting in memory*. In other
words, I can always perform any recollection

whatsoever in the personal mode, and at once the *I* appears. Such is the *factual* guarantee of the Kantian claim *concerning validity*. Thus it seems that there is not one of my consciousnesses which I do not apprehend as provided with an *I*.

But it must be remembered that all the writers who have described the *Cogito* have dealt with it as a reflective operation, that is to say, as an operation of the second degree. Such a *Cogito* is performed by a consciousness *directed upon consciousness*, a consciousness which takes consciousness as an object. Let us agree: the certitude of the *Cogito* is absolute, for, as Husserl said, there is an indissoluble unity of the reflecting consciousness and the reflected consciousness (to the point that the reflecting consciousness could not exist without the reflected consciousness). But the fact remains that we are in the presence of a synthesis of two consciousnesses, one of which is consciousness *of* the other. Thus the essential principle of phenomenology, "all consciousness is consciousness *of* something," [13] is preserved. Now, my reflecting consciousness does not take itself for an object when I effect the *Cogito*. What it affirms concerns the reflected consciousness. Insofar as my reflecting consciousness is consciousness of itself,

it is *non-positional* consciousness. It becomes positional only by directing itself upon the reflected consciousness which itself was not a positional consciousness of itself before being reflected. Thus the consciousness which says *I Think* is precisely not the consciousness which thinks. Or rather it is not *its own* thought which it posits by this thetic act. We are then justified in asking ourselves if the *I* which thinks is common to the two superimposed consciousnesses, or if it is not rather the *I* of the reflected consciousness. All reflecting consciousness is, indeed, in itself unreflected, and a new act of the third degree is necessary in order to posit it. Moreover, there is no infinite regress here, since a consciousness has no need at all of a reflecting consciousness in order to be conscious of itself. It simply does not posit itself as an object.

But is it not precisely the reflective act which gives birth to the *me* in the reflected consciousness? Thus would be explained how every thought apprehended by intuition possesses an *I*, without falling into the difficulties noted in the preceding section. Husserl would be the first to acknowledge that an unreflected thought undergoes a radical modification in becoming reflected. But need one confine this modification to a loss of "naïveté"? Would not the appearance of the *I* be what is essential in this change?

One must evidently revert to a concrete experience, which may seem impossible, since by definition such an experience is reflective, that is to say, supplied with an *I*. But every unreflected consciousness, being non-thetic consciousness of itself, leaves a non-thetic memory that one can consult. To do so it suffices to try to reconstitute the complete moment in which this unreflected consciousness appeared (which by definition is always possible). For example, I was absorbed just now in my reading. I am going to try to remember the circumstances of my reading, my attitude, the lines that I was reading. I am thus going to revive not only these external details but a certain depth of unreflected consciousness, since the objects could only have been perceived *by* that consciousness and since they remain relative to it. That consciousness must not be posited as object of a reflection. On the contrary, I must direct my attention to the revived objects, but *without losing sight of the unreflected consciousness*, by joining in a sort of conspiracy with it and by drawing up an inventory of its content in a non-positional manner. There is no doubt about the result: while I was reading, there was consciousness *of* the book, *of* the heroes of the novel, but the *I* was not inhabiting this consciousness. It was only consciousness of the object and non-positional consciousness of itself. I can now make these a-thetically apprehended results the object of a thesis and declare: there was no *I* in the unreflected consciousness. It should not be thought that this operation is artificial or conceived for the needs of the case. Thanks to this operation, evidently, Titchener could say in his *Textbook of Psychology*[14] that the *me* was very often absent from his consciousness. He went no further, however, and did not attempt to classify the states of consciousness lacking a *me*.

It is undoubtedly tempting to object that this operation, this non-reflective apprehension of one consciousness by another consciousness, can evidently take place only by memory, and that therefore it does not profit from the absolute certitude inherent in a reflective act. We would then find ourselves, *on the one hand*, with an absolutely certain act which permits the presence of the *I* in the reflected consciousness to be affirmed, and, *on the other hand*, with a questionable memory which would purport to show the absence of the

I from the unreflected consciousness. It would seem that we have no right to oppose the latter to the former. But I must point out that the memory of the unreflected consciousness is not opposed to the data of the reflective consciousness. No one would deny for a moment that the *I* appears in a reflected consciousness. It is simply a question of opposing a reflective memory of my reading ("I was reading"), which is itself of a questionable nature, to a non-reflective memory. The validity of a present reflection, in fact, does not reach beyond the consciousness presently apprehended. And reflective memory, to which we are obliged to have recourse in order to reinstate elapsed consciousnesses, besides its questionable character owing to its nature as memory, remains suspect since, in the opinion of Husserl himself, reflection *modifies* the spontaneous consciousness. Since, in consequence, all the non-reflective memories of unreflected consciousness show me a consciousness *without a me*, and since, on the other hand, theoretical considerations concerning consciousness which are based on intuition of essence have constrained us to recognize[15] that the *I* cannot be a part of the internal structure of *Erlebnisse*, we must therefore conclude: there is no *I* on the unreflected level. When I run after a

streetcar, when I look at the time, when I am
absorbed in contemplating a portrait, there is no
I. There is consciousness *of the streetcar-having-
to-be-overtaken*, etc., and non-positional consciousness of consciousness. In fact, I am then
plunged into the world of objects; it is they
which constitute the unity of my consciousnesses; it is they which present themselves with
values, with attractive and repellant qualities—
but *me*, I have disappeared; I have annihilated
myself. There is no place for *me* on this level.
And this is not a matter of chance, due to a mo-
mentary lapse of attention, but happens because
of the very structure of consciousness.

This is what a description of the *Cogito* will
make even more obvious to us. Can one say, indeed, that the reflective act apprehends the *I*
and the thinking consciousness to the same degree and in the same way? Husserl insists on the
fact that the certitude of the reflective act comes
from apprehending consciousness without facets,
without profiles, completely (without *Abschattungen*). This is evidently so. On the contrary,
the spatio-temporal object always manifests itself
through an infinity of aspects and is, at bottom,
only the ideal unity of this infinity. As for meanings, or eternal truths, they affirm their tran-

scendence in that the moment they appear they are given as independent of time, whereas the consciousness which apprehends them is, on the contrary, individuated through and through in duration. Now we ask: when a reflective consciousness apprehends the *I Think*, does it apprehend a full and concrete consciousness gathered into a real moment of concrete duration? The reply is clear: the *I* is not given as a concrete moment, a perishable structure of my actual consciousness. On the contrary, it affirms its permanence beyond this consciousness and all consciousnesses, and—although it scarcely resembles a mathematical truth—its type of existence comes much nearer to that of eternal truths than to that of consciousness.

Indeed, it is obvious that Descartes passed from the *Cogito* to the idea of thinking substance because he believed that *I* and *think* are on the same level. We have just seen that Husserl, although less obviously, is ultimately subject to the same reproach. I quite recognize that Husserl grants to the *I* a special transcendence which is not the transcendence of the object, and which one could call a transcendence "from above." But by what right? And how account for this privileged treatment of the *I* if not by metaphysi-

cal and Critical preoccupations which have nothing to do with phenomenology? Let us be more
radical and assert without fear that *all transcendence* must fall under the ἐποχή; thus, perhaps, we shall avoid writing such awkward
chapters as Section Sixty-one of *Ideen Zu Einer
Reinen Phänomenologischen Philosophie.*[16] If the
I in the *I think* affirms itself as transcendent, this
is because the *I* is not of the same nature as transcendental consciousness.

Let us also note that the *I Think* does not appear to reflection as the reflected consciousness:
it is given *through* reflected consciousness. To be
sure, it is apprehended by intuition and is an object grasped with evidence. But we know what a
service Husserl has rendered to philosophy by
distinguishing diverse kinds of evidence. Well, it
is only too certain that the *I* of the *I Think* is an
object grasped with neither apodictic nor adequate evidence.[17] The evidence is not apodictic,
since by saying *I* we affirm far more than we
know. It is not adequate, for the *I* is presented as
an opaque reality whose content would have to
be unfolded. To be sure, the *I* manifests itself as
the source of consciousness. But that alone should
make us pause. Indeed, for this very reason the *I*
appears veiled, indistinct through consciousness,

like a pebble at the bottom of the water. For this very reason the *I* is deceptive from the start, since we know that nothing but consciousness can be the source of consciousness.

In addition, if the *I* is a part of consciousness, there would then be *two I*'s: the *I* of the reflective consciousness and the *I* of the reflected consciousness. Fink, the disciple of Husserl, is even acquainted with a third *I*, disengaged by the ἐποχή, the *I* of transcendental consciousness. Hence the problem of the three *I*'s, whose difficulties Fink agreeably mentions.[18] For us, this problem is quite simply insoluble. For it is inadmissible that any communication could be established between the reflective *I* and the reflected *I* if they are real elements of consciousness; above all, it is inadmissible that they may finally achieve identity in one unique *I*.

By way of conclusion to this analysis, it seems to me that one can make the following statements:

First, the *I* is an *existent*. It has a concrete type of existence, undoubtedly different from the existence of mathematical truths, of meanings, or of spatio-temporal beings, but no less real. The *I* gives itself as transcendent.

Second, the *I* proffers itself to an intuition of a special kind[19] which apprehends it, always inadequately, behind the reflected consciousness.

Third, the *I* never appears except on the occasion of a reflective act. In this case, the complex structure of consciousness is as follows: there is an unreflected act of reflection, without an *I*, which is directed on a reflected consciousness. The latter becomes the object of the reflecting consciousness without ceasing to affirm its own object (a chair, a mathematical truth, etc.). At the same time, a new object appears which is the occasion for an affirmation by reflective consciousness, and which is consequently not on the same level as the unreflected consciousness (because the latter consciousness is an absolute which has no need of reflective consciousness in order to exist), nor on the same level as the object of the reflected consciousness (chair, etc.). This transcendent object of the reflective act is the *I*.

Fourth, the transcendent *I* must fall before the stroke of phenomenological reduction. The *Cogito* affirms too much. The certain content of the pseudo-"Cogito" is not "*I have* consciousness of this chair," but "There is consciousness of this chair." This content is sufficient to constitute an infinite and absolute field of investigation for phenomenology.

C.   THE THEORY OF THE MATERIAL PRESENCE OF THE *Me*

For Kant and for Husserl the *I* is a formal structure of consciousness. We have tried to show that an *I* is never purely formal, that it is always, even when conceived abstractly, an infinite contraction of the material *me*. But before going further we need to free ourselves of a purely psychological theory which for psychological reasons affirms the material presence of the *me* in all our consciousnesses. This is the theory of the "self-love" moralists. According to them, the love of self—and consequently the *me*—lies concealed within all emotions in a thousand different forms. In a very general way, the *me*, as a function of this love that it bears for itself, would desire *for itself* all the objects it desires. The essential structure of each of my acts would be a *reference to myself*. The "return to me" would be constitutive of all consciousnesses.

To object to this thesis that this return to **my-**

self is nowise present to consciousness—for example, to object that, when I am thirsty, it is a glass of water which I see and which appears to me as desirable—raises no issue. This point would willingly be granted. La Rochefoucauld was one of the first to have made use of the unconscious, without naming it. For him, self-love *conceals itself* under the most diverse forms. It must be ferreted out before it can be grasped. In a more general way, it has been admitted as a consequence that the *me*, if it is not present to consciousness, is hidden behind consciousness and is the magnetic pole of all our representations and all our desires. The *me* seeks, then, to procure the object in order to satisfy its desire. In other words, it is the desire (or, if one prefers, the desiring *me*) which is given as end, and the desired object is the means.

Now the interest of this thesis, it seems to us, is that it puts in bold relief a very frequent error among psychologists. The error consists in confusing the essential structure of reflective acts with the essential structure of unreflected acts. It is overlooked that two forms of existence are always possible for a consciousness. Then, each time the observed consciousnesses are given as unreflected, one superimposes on them a structure, belonging to reflection, which one doggedly alleges to be unconscious.

I pity Peter, and I go to his assistance. For my consciousness only one thing exists at that moment: Peter-having-to-be-helped. This quality of "having-to-be-helped" lies in Peter. It acts on me like a force. Aristotle said it: the desirable is that which moves the desiring. At this level, the desire is given to consciousness as centrifugal (it transcends itself; it is thetic consciousness of "having-to-be" and non-thetic consciousness of itself) and as impersonal (there is no *me:* I am in the presence of Peter's suffering just as I am in the presence of the color of this inkstand; there is an objective world of things and of actions, done or to be done, and the actions come to adhere as qualities to the things which call for them).

Now, this first moment of desire—supposing that it has not completely escaped the self-love theorists—is not considered a complete and autonomous moment. They have imagined another state behind it which remains in a half-light: for example, I help Peter in order to put an end to the disagreeable state into which the sight of his sufferings has put me. But this disagreeable state can be known as such, and one can try to suppress it only following an act of reflection. A distaste on the unreflected level, in fact, transcends itself in the same way that the unreflected consciousness of pity transcends itself. It is the intuitive apprehension of a disagreeable quality of an object. And to the extent that the distaste is accompanied by a desire, it does not desire to suppress *itself*, but to suppress the unpleasant object. It is therefore no use to place behind the unreflected pitying consciousness an unpleasant state which is to be made the underlying cause of the pitying act: for unless this consciousness of unpleasantness turns back on itself in order to posit itself as an unpleasant state, we will remain indefinitely in the impersonal and unreflected. Thus, without even realizing it, the self-love theorists suppose that the reflected is first, original, and concealed in the unconscious. There is scarcely need to bring to light the absurdity of such a hypothesis. Even if the unconscious exists, who could be led to believe that it contains spontaneities of a reflected sort? Is it not the definition of the reflected that it be posited by a consciousness? But, in addition, how can it be held that the reflected is first in relation to the unreflected? Undoubtedly, one can conceive that in certain cases a consciousness may appear immediately as reflected. But even then the unre-

flected has the ontological priority over the reflected because the unreflected consciousness
does not need to be reflected in order to exist,
and because reflection presupposes the interven-
tion of a second-degree consciousness.

We arrive then at the following conclusion:
unreflected consciousness must be considered
autonomous. It is a totality which needs no com-
pleting at all, and we must acknowledge with no
qualifications that the character of unreflected
desire is to transcend itself by apprehending on
the subject the quality of desirability. Everything
happens as if we lived in a world whose objects,
in addition to their qualities of warmth, odor,
shape, etc., had the qualities of repulsive, attractive, delightful, useful, etc., and as if these qualities were forces having a certain power over us.
In the case of reflection, and only in that case,
affectivity is posited for itself, as desire, fear, etc.
Only in the case of reflection can I think "*I* hate
Peter," "*I* pity Paul," etc.

Contrary to what has been held, therefore, it is
on the reflected level that the ego-life has its
place, and on the unreflected level that the impersonal life has its place (which naturally does
not mean that all reflected life is necessarily
egoistic, or that all unreflected life is necessarily

altruistic). Reflection "poisons" desire. On the unreflected level I bring Peter help because Peter is "having to be helped." But if my state is suddenly transformed into a reflected state, there I am watching myself act, in the sense in which one says of someone that he listens to himself talk. It is no longer Peter who attracts me, it is *my* helpful consciousness which appears to me as having to be perpetuated. Even if I only think that I must pursue my action because "that is good," the good qualifies *my* conduct, *my* pity, etc. The psychology of La Rochefoucauld has its place. And yet this psychology is not *true:* it is not my fault if my reflective life poisons "by its very essence" my spontaneous life. Before being "poisoned" my desires were pure. It is the point of view that I have taken toward them which has poisoned them. The psychology of La Rochefoucauld is true only for particular emotions which have their origin in reflective life, that is to say, which are given first as *my emotions,* instead of first transcending themselves toward an object.

Thus a purely psychological examination of "intra-mundane" consciousness leads us to the same conclusions as our phenomenological study: the *me* must not be sought *in* the states of unreflected consciousness, nor *behind* them. The *me* appears only with the reflective act, and as a noematic correlate[20] of a reflective intention. We begin to get a glimpse of the fact that the *I* and the *me* are only one. We are going to try to show that this ego, of which *I* and *me* are but two aspects, constitutes the ideal and indirect (noematic) unity of the infinite series of our reflected consciousnesses.

The *I* is the ego as the unity of actions. The *me* is the ego as the unity of states and of qualities. The distinction that one makes between these two aspects of one and the same reality seems to us simply functional, not to say grammatical.

ii   the constitution of the ego

The ego is not directly the unity of reflected consciousnesses. There exists an *immanent* unity of these consciousnesses: the flux of consciousness constituting itself as the unity of itself.[21] And there exists a *transcendent* unity: states and actions. The ego is the unity of states and of actions —optionally, of qualities. It is the unity of transcendent unities, and itself transcendent. It is a transcendent pole of synthetic unity, like the object-pole of the unreflected attitude, except that this pole appears solely in the world of reflection.

We shall examine successively the constitution of *states*, of *actions*, and of *qualities*, and the appearance of the *me* as the pole of these transcendences.

A. STATES AS TRANSCENDENT UNITIES OF CONSCIOUSNESS

The *state* appears to reflective consciousness. The state is given to it, and is the object of a concrete intuition. If I hate Peter, my hatred of Peter is a state that I can apprehend by reflection. This state is *present* to the gaze of reflective consciousness. It is *real*.

Is it therefore necessary to conclude that the state is immanent and certain? Surely not. We must not make of reflection a mysterious and infallible power, nor believe that everything reflection attains is indubitable *because* attained by reflection. Reflection has limits, both limits of validity and limits in fact. It is a consciousness which posits a consciousness. Everything that it affirms regarding this consciousness is certain and adequate. But if other objects appear to it through this consciousness, there is no reason that these objects should participate in the characteristics of consciousness. Let us consider a reflective experience of hatred. I see Peter, I feel a sort of profound convulsion of repugnance and anger at the sight of him (I am already on the reflective level): the convulsion is consciousness. I cannot be mistaken when I say: I feel at this moment a violent repugnance for Peter. But is this experience of repugnance hatred? Obviously not. Moreover, it is not given as such. In reality, I have hated Peter a long time and I think that I shall hate him always. An instantaneous consciousness of repugnance could not, then, be my hatred. If I limited it to what it is, to something instantaneous, I could not even speak of hatred anymore. I would say: "I feel a repugnance for Peter at this moment," and thus I would not implicate the future. But precisely by this refusal to implicate the future, I would cease to hate.

Now my hatred appears to me at the same time as my experience of repugnance. But it appears *through* this experience. It is given precisely as

not being limited to this experience. My hatred was given *in* and *by* each movement of disgust, of repugnance, and of anger, but at the same time it *is not* any of them. My hatred escapes from each of them by affirming its permanence. It affirms that it had already appeared when I thought about Peter with so much fury yesterday, and that it will appear tomorrow. It effects by itself, moreover, a distinction between *to be* and *to appear*, since it gives itself as continuing *to be* even when I am absorbed in other occupations and no consciousness reveals it. This is enough, it would seem, to enable us to affirm that hatred is not *of* consciousness. It overflows the instantaneousness of consciousness, and it does not bow to the absolute law of consciousness for which no distinction is possible between appearance and being. Hatred, then, is a transcendent object. Each *Erlebnis* reveals it as a whole, but at the same time the *Erlebnis* is a profile, a projection (an *Abschattung*). Hatred is credit for an infinity of angry or repulsed consciousnesses in the past and in the future. It is the transcendent unity of this infinity of consciousnesses. Thus, to say "I hate" or "I love" on the occasion of a particular consciousness of attraction or repugnance is to effect a veritable passage to infinity, rather analogous to that which we effect when we perceive *an* inkstand, or *the blue* of the blotter.

No more is needed in order for the rights of reflection to be singularly limited. It is certain that Peter is repugnant to me. But it is and always will remain doubtful that I hate him. Indeed, this affirmation infinitely exceeds the power of reflection. Naturally, one need not therefore conclude that hatred is a mere hypothesis, an empty concept: it is indeed a real object which I am apprehending through the *Erlebnis*. But this object is outside consciousness, and the very nature of its existence implies its "dubitability." Reflection too has its certain domain and its doubtful domain, a sphere of adequate evidence and a sphere of inadequate evidence. Pure reflection (which, however, is not necessarily phenomenological reflection) keeps to the given without setting up claims for the future. This can be seen when someone, after having said in anger, "I detest you," catches himself and says, "It is not true, I do not detest you, I said that in anger." We see here two reflections: the one, impure and conniving, which effects then and there a passage to the infinite, and which through the *Erlebnis* abruptly constitutes hatred as its transcendent object; the other, pure, merely descriptive, which

disarms the unreflected consciousness by grant-
ing its instantaneousness. These two reflections
apprehend the same, certain data, but the one
affirms *more* than it knows, directing itself
through the reflected consciousness upon an object situated outside consciousness.

As soon as one leaves the domain of pure or
impure reflection and meditates on the results of
reflection, one is tempted to confuse the transcendent meaning of the *Erlebnis* with its character as immanent. This confusion leads the psy-
chologist to two types of error. Because I am
often mistaken about my emotions—because, for
example, I come to believe I love when I hate—I
may conclude that introspection is deceptive. In
this case I definitively separate my *state* from its
appearances. I hold that a symbolical interpretation of all appearances (considered as symbols)
is necessary in order to determine the emotion,
and I assume a relation of causality between the
emotion and its appearances. Now the unconscious re-emerges. Or else, because I know on the
contrary that my introspection is sound, that I
cannot doubt my consciousness of repugnance so
long as I have it, I think I am entitled to transfer
this certitude to the emotion. I thus conclude that
my hatred can shut itself up in the immanence

and adequation of an instantaneous consciousness.

Hatred is a *state*. And by this term I have tried
to express the character of passivity which is constitutive of hatred. Undoubtedly it will be said
that hatred is a force, an irresistible drive, etc.
But an electric current or the fall of water are
also forces to be reckoned with: does this diminish one whit the passivity and inertia of their
nature? Is it any less the case that they receive
their energy *from the outside?* The passivity of a
spatio-temporal thing is constituted by virtue of
its existential relativity. A relative existence can
only be passive, since the least activity would
free it from the relative and would constitute it as
absolute. In the same way, hatred is *inert*, since it
is existence relative to reflective consciousness.
And, naturally, in speaking of the inertia of hatred we mean to say nothing if not that hatred
appears so to consciousness. In fact, do we not
say, "My hatred was reawakened," "His hatred
was combated by the violent desire to . . . ," etc.?
Are not the struggles of hatred against morality,
censure, etc., represented as conflicts of *physical*
forces to the point even that Balzac and most of
the novelists (sometimes Proust himself) attribute to states the principle of independent forces?

The whole psychology of states (and non-phe-
nomenological psychology in general) is a psychology of the inert.

The state is given as a kind of intermediary between the body (the immediate "thing") and the
Erlebnis. Only it is not given as acting in the
same way on the bodily side and on the side of
consciousness. On the side of the body, its action
is unmitigatedly causal. It is the cause of my act
of mimicry, of my gestures. "Why were you so
unpleasant to Peter? *Because* I detest him." But
it cannot be the same (save in theories constructed *a priori* and with empty concepts, like
Freudianism) on the side of consciousness. In no
case, indeed, can reflection be mistaken about
the spontaneity of the reflected consciousness:
this is the domain of reflective certitude. Also,
the relation between hatred and the "instantaneous" consciousness of disgust is constructed in
such a way as to take care of both the exigencies
of hatred (to be first, to be the *origin*) and the
certain data of reflection (spontaneity), for the
consciousness of disgust appears to reflection as
a spontaneous emanation from hatred.

We observe here for the first time this notion
of *emanation*, which is so important whenever
there is a question of connecting the inert psy-

chical states to the spontaneities of consciousness.
Repugnance is given, in some way, as producing
itself *at the instance of* the hatred and *at the ex-
pense of* the hatred. Hatred appears through the
consciousness of disgust as that from which the
latter emanates. We readily acknowledge that
the relation of the hatred to the particular
Erlebnis of repugnance is not logical. It is a
magical bond, assuredly. But we have aimed
only at describing. Moreover, we will soon see
that it is exclusively in magical terms that we
should speak of the relations of the *me* to consciousness.

B.   THE CONSTITUTION OF ACTIONS

We shall not attempt to establish the distinction
between *active* consciousness and simply spontaneous consciousness. Moreover, it seems to us
that this is one of the most difficult problems of
phenomenology. We would simply like to remark that concerted action is first of all (whatever the nature of the active consciousness may
be) a transcendent. That is obvious for actions
like "playing the piano," "driving a car," "writ-

ing," because these actions are "taken" in the world of things. But purely psychical actions like doubting, reasoning, meditating, making a hypothesis, these too must be conceived as transcendences. What deceives us here is that action is not only the noematic[22] unity of a stream of consciousnesses: it is also a concrete realization. But we must not forget that action requires time to be accomplished. It has articulations; it has moments. To these moments correspond concrete, active consciousnesses, and the reflection which is directed on the consciousnesses apprehends the total action in an intuition which exhibits it as the transcendent unity of the active consciousnesses. In this sense, one can say that the spontaneous doubt which invades me when I glimpse an object in the shadows is a *consciousness*, but the methodological doubt of Descartes is an action, that is to say, a transcendent object of reflective consciousness. Here one sees the danger: when Descartes says, "I doubt therefore I am," is this a matter of the spontaneous doubt that reflective consciousness apprehends in its instantaneousness, or is this precisely a matter of the enterprise of doubting? This ambiguity, we have seen, may be the origin of serious errors.

The ego, we shall see, is directly the transcendent unity of states and of actions. Nevertheless there can exist an intermediary between actions and states: the quality. When we have experienced hatred several times toward different persons, or tenacious resentments, or protracted angers, we unify these diverse manifestations by intending a psychic disposition for producing them. This psychic disposition (I am very spiteful, I am capable of hating violently, I am ill-tempered) is naturally more and other than a mere contrivance. It is a transcendent object. It represents the substratum of the states, as the states represent the substratum of the *Erlebnisse*. But its relation with the emotions is not a relation of emanation. Emanation only connects consciousnesses to psychic passivities. The relation of the quality to the state (or to the action) is a relation of actualization. The quality is given as a potentiality, a virtuality, which, under the influence[23] of diverse factors, can pass into actuality. Its actuality is precisely the state (or the action). We see the essential difference between the quality and the state. The state is a noematic unity of spontaneities. The quality is a unity of objective passivities. In the absence of any consciousness of hatred, hatred is given as actually existing. On the contrary, in the absence of any feeling of spite, the corresponding quality remains a potentiality. Potentiality is not mere possibility: it presents itself as something which really exists, but its mode of existence is potency. Naturally, faults, virtues, tastes, talents, tendencies, instincts, etc., are of this type. These unifications are always possible. The influence of preconceived ideas and of social factors is here preponderant. Concomitantly, such unifications are never indispensable, because states and actions can find directly in the ego the unity that they demand.

D. THE CONSTITUTION OF THE EGO AS THE POLE OF
   ACTIONS, STATES, AND QUALITIES

We have been learning to distinguish "the psychic" from consciousness. The psychic is the transcendent object of reflective consciousness.[24] It is also the object of the science called "psychology." The ego appears to reflection as a transcendent object effecting the permanent synthesis of the psychic. The ego is *on the side of* the psychic. Let us note here that the ego that we are considering is psychic, not psycho-physical. It is not by abstraction that we separate these two aspects of the ego. The psycho-physical *me* is a synthetic enrichment of the psychic ego, which can very well (and without reduction of any sort) exist in a free state. It is certain, for example, that when we say "I am undecided," we do not directly refer to the psycho-physical *me*.

It would be tempting to constitute the ego as a "subject-pole" like that "object-pole" which Husserl places at the center of the noematic nucleus. This object-pole is an X which supports determinations:

Predicates, however, are predicates of "something." This something also belongs to the nucleus in question and obviously cannot be separated from the nucleus. It is the central point of unity of which we were speaking earlier. It is the point of attachment for predicates, their support. But in no respect is it a unity of the predicates in the sense of some complex, in the sense of some linkage of predicates. It is necessarily to be distinguished from predicates, even if one cannot set it beside them, nor separate it from them; just as they are its predicates, un-

thinkable without it and yet distinguishable from it.[25]

By that Husserl means to indicate that he considers things as syntheses which are at least ideally analyzable. Undoubtedly, this tree, this table are synthetic complexes and each quality is tied to every other. But each is tied to each *in so far as each quality belongs to the same object*, X. What is logically first are unilateral relations by which each quality belongs (directly or indirectly) to this X like a predicate to a subject. It follows that an analysis is always possible.

This notion is most debatable, but this is not the place to examine it. What matters to us is that an indissoluble synthetic totality which could support itself would have no need of a supporting X, provided of course that it were really and concretely unanalyzable. If we take a melody, for example, it is useless to presuppose an X which would serve as a support for the different notes. The unity here comes from the absolute indissolubility of the elements which cannot be conceived as separated, save by abstraction. The subject of the predicate here will be the concrete totality, and the predicate will be a quality abstractly separated from the totality, a quality which has its full meaning only if one connects it again to the totality.[26]

For these very reasons we shall not permit ourselves to see the ego as a sort of X-pole which would be the support of psychic phenomena. Such an X would, by definition, be indifferent to the psychic qualities it would support. But the ego, as we shall see, is never indifferent to its states; it is "compromised" by them. Now, to be exact, a support can be thus compromised by what it supports only in case it is a concrete totality which supports and contains its own qualities. The ego is nothing outside of the concrete totality of states and actions it supports. Undoubtedly it is transcendent to all the states which it unifies, but not as an abstract X whose mission is only to unify: rather, it is the infinite totality of states and of actions which is never reducible to *an* action or to *a* state. If we were to seek for unreflected consciousness an analogue of what the ego is for consciousness of the second degree, we rather believe that it would be necessary to think of the *World*, conceived as the infinite synthetic totality of all things. Sometimes we do, in fact, apprehend the World beyond our immediate surroundings as a vast concrete existence. In this case, the things which surround us appear only as the extreme point of this World which surpasses them and envelops them. The ego is to psychical objects what the World is to things. But the appearance of the World in the background of things is rather rare; special circumstances, described very well by Heidegger in *Sein und Zeit*,[27] are necessary for it to "reveal" itself. The ego, on the contrary, always appears at the horizon of states. Each state, each action is given as incapable of being separated from the ego without abstraction. And if judgment separates the *I* from its state (as in the phrase: *I* am in love), this can be only in order to bind them at once. The movement of separation would end in an empty and false meaning if it were not given as incomplete, and if it did not complete itself by a movement of synthesis.

This transcendent totality participates in the questionable character of all transcendence. This is to say that everything given to us by our intuitions of the ego is always given as capable of being contradicted by subsequent intuitions. For example, I can see clearly that I am ill-tempered, jealous, etc., and nevertheless I may be mistaken. In other words, I may deceive myself in thinking that I have *such* a *me*. The error, moreover, is not committed on the level of judgment, but already on the level of pre-judgmental evidence.[28] This questionable character of my ego—or even the intuitional error that I commit—does not signify that I have a *true me* which I am unaware of, but only that the intended ego has in itself the character of dubitability (in certain cases, the character of falsehood). The metaphysical hypothesis according to which my ego would not be composed of elements having existed in reality (ten years ago or a second ago), but would only be constituted of false memories, is not excluded. The power of the *malin génie* extends so far.

But if it is in the nature of the ego to be a dubitable object, it does not follow that the ego is *hypothetical*. In fact, the ego is the spontaneous, transcendent unification of our states and our actions. In this capacity, it is no hypothesis. I do not say to myself, "Perhaps I have an ego," as I may say to myself, "Perhaps I hate Peter." I do not seek here a unifying *meaning* of my states. When I unify my consciousnesses under the title "hatred," I add a certain meaning to them, I qualify them. But when I incorporate my states in the concrete totality *me*, I add nothing to them. In reality, the relation of the ego to the qualities, states, and actions is neither a relation of emanation (like the relation of consciousness to emotion), nor a relation of actualization (like the relation of the quality to the state). It is a relation on the order of poetic production (in the sense of ποιειν), or if you like, a relation of creation.

Everyone, by consulting the results of his intuition, can observe that the ego is given as producing its states. We undertake here a description of this transcendent ego such as it reveals itself in intuition.

We begin therefore with this undeniable fact: each new state is fastened directly (or indirectly, by the quality) to the ego, as to its origin. This mode of creation is indeed a creation *ex nihilo*, in the sense that the state is not given as having formerly been in the *me*.

Even if hatred is given as the actualization of a certain power of spite or hatred, it remains something new in relation to the power it actualizes. Thus the unifying act of reflection fastens each new state, in a very special way, to the concrete totality, *me*. Reflection is not confined to apprehending the new state as attaching to this totality, as fusing with it: reflection intends a relation which traverses time backwards and which gives the *me* as the source of the state.

The same is true, naturally, for actions in relation to the *I*. As for qualities, although *qualifying* the *me*, they are not given as something by virtue of which the *me* exists (as is the case, for example, for an aggregate: each stone, each brick exists through itself, and their aggregate exists by virtue of each of them). But, on the contrary, the ego maintains its qualities through a genuine, continuous creation. Nevertheless, we do not finally apprehend the ego as a pure creative source beside the qualities. It does not seem to us that we could find a skeletal pole if we took away, one after the other, all the qualities. If the ego appears as beyond each quality, or even as beyond all qualities, this is because the ego is opaque like an object: we would have to undertake an infinite plundering in order to take away all its powers. And, at the end of this plundering, nothing would remain; the ego would have vanished. The ego is the creator of its states and sustains its qualities in existence by a sort of preserving spontaneity. We must not confuse this creative or preserving spontaneity with Responsibility, which is a special case of creative production on the part of the ego. It would be interesting to study the diverse types of progression from the ego to its states. Most of the time, the progression involved is magical. At other times, it may be rational (in the case of reflective will, for example). But always there is a ground of unintelligibility, for which we shall give the reason later. According to different consciousnesses (prelogical, childish, schizophrenic, logical, etc.), the nuance of the creation varies, but always it remains a poetic production. A very peculiar case of considerable interest is that of psychoses of influence. What does the sick person mean by these words: "They *make me* have evil thoughts"? We shall attempt a study of this in another work.[29] Let us remark here, however, that the spontaneity of the ego is not negated: it is in some way *spellbound*, but it remains.

But this spontaneity must not be confused with the spontaneity of consciousness. Indeed, the ego, being an object, is *passive*. It is a question, therefore, of a pseudo-spontaneity which is suitably symbolized by the spurting of a spring, a geyser, etc. This is to say that we are dealing here with a semblance only. Genuine spontaneity must be perfectly clear: it *is* what it produces and can be nothing else. If it were tied synthetically to something other than itself, it would in fact embrace some obscurity, and even a certain passivity, in the transformation. Indeed, it would be necessary to admit a passage from *itself* to *something else*, which would presuppose that spontaneity escapes from itself. The spontaneity of the ego does escape from itself, since the hatred of the ego, although unable to exist quite by itself, possesses in spite of everything a certain independence with respect to the ego. So that the ego is always surpassed by what it produces, although, from another point of view, it *is* what it produces. Hence the classic surprises: "*I*, I could do that!"—"*I*, I could hate my father!"— etc. Here, evidently, the concrete totality of the *me* intuited up to this time weighs down the productive *I* and holds it back a little from what the *I* has just produced. The linkage of the ego to its states remains, therefore, an unintelligible spontaneity. This is the spontaneity described by Bergson in *Essai sur les Données Immédiates de la Conscience*,[30] which he took for freedom, without realizing that he was describing an *object* rather than a consciousness, and that the union posited is perfectly irrational because the producer is passive with respect to the created thing.

However irrational it may be, this union is nonetheless the union noted in our intuition of the ego. And this is its meaning: the ego is an object apprehended, but also an object *constituted*,

by reflective consciousness. The ego is a virtual locus of unity, and consciousness constitutes it in *a direction contrary to* that actually taken by the production: *really*, consciousnesses are first; through these are constituted states; and then, through the latter, the ego is constituted. But, as the order is reversed by a consciousness which imprisons itself in the world in order to flee from itself, consciousnesses are given as emanating from states, and states as produced by the ego. It follows that consciousness projects its own spontaneity into the ego-object in order to confer on the ego the creative power which is absolutely necessary to it. But this spontaneity, *represented* and *hypostatized* in an object, becomes a degraded and bastard spontaneity, which magically preserves its creative power even while becoming passive. Whence the profound irrationality of the notion of an ego.

We are familiar with other degraded aspects of conscious spontaneity. I cite only one of these: expressive and able mimicry can present us with the *Erlebnis* of our interlocutor in all its meaning, all its nuances, all its freshness. But it is given to us *degraded*, that is to say, *passive*. We are thus surrounded by magical objects which retain, as it were, a memory of the spontaneity of consciousness, yet continue to be objects of the world. This is why man is always a sorcerer for man. Indeed, this poetic connection of two passivities in which one creates the other spontaneously is the very foundation of sorcery, the profound meaning of "participation." This is also why we are sorcerers for ourselves each time we view our *me*.

By virtue of this passivity the ego is capable of being *affected*. Nothing can act on consciousness, because it is cause of itself. But, on the contrary, the ego which produces undergoes the reverberation of what it produces. The ego is "compromised" by what it produces. Here a relation reverses itself: the action or the state returns upon the ego to qualify it. This leads us again to the relation of "participation." Each new state produced by the ego colors and tinges the ego slightly the moment the ego produces it. The ego is in some way spellbound by this action, it "participates" with it. It was not the crime of Raskolnikoff which was incorporated into his ego. Or rather, to be exact, it was the crime, but in a condensed form, in the form of a "killing bruise." [31] Thus everything that the ego produces affects it. We must add: *and only* what it produces. One might object that the *me* can be transformed by external events (catastrophe, mourning, trickery, change in social environment, etc.). But this is so only insofar as external events are for the *me* the occasion of states or actions. Everything happens as if the ego were protected by its phantom-like spontaneity from any direct contact with the outside, as if it could communicate with the World only by the intermediary of states or actions. We see the reason for this isolation: quite simply, the ego is an object which appears only to reflection, and which is thereby radically cut off from the World. The ego does not live on the same level.

Just as the ego is an irrational synthesis of activity and passivity, it is a synthesis of interiority and transcendence. It is, in a sense, more "internal to" consciousness than are states. This is precisely the interiority of the reflected consciousness, contemplated by the reflective consciousness. But one could easily suppose this to mean that reflection makes interiority into an object by *contemplation*. Yet what do we mean by "interiority"? Simply that to be and to be aware of itself are one and the same thing for consciousness. This may be expressed in different ways: I may say, for example, that for consciousness appearance is the absolute to the extent that it **is** appearance; or, again, that consciousness is a being whose essence involves its existence. These diverse formulations permit us to conclude that one *lives* interiority (that one *"exists inward"*), but that one does not contemplate it, since interiority would itself be beyond contemplation, as its condition.

It would be no use to object that reflection posits the reflected consciousness and thereby its interiority. The case is a special one: reflection and reflected are only one, as Husserl has very well shown, and the interiority of the one fuses with that of the other. To posit interiority before oneself, however, is necessarily to give it the load of an object. This transpires as if interiority closed upon itself and proffered us only its outside; as if one had to "circle about" it in order to understand it. And this is just how the ego gives itself to reflection: as an interiority closed upon itself. It is inward *for itself, not for consciousness*. Naturally, we are dealing with a contradictory composite: for an absolute interiority never has an outside. It can be conceived only by itself, and that is why we cannot apprehend the consciousnesses of others (for that reason only, and not because bodies separate us).

In reality, this degraded and irrational interi-

ority may be analyzed into two very special
structures: *intimacy* and *indistinctness*. In relation to consciousness, the ego is given as intimate. Everything happens as though the ego
were *of* consciousness, with only this particular
and essential difference: that the ego is opaque
to consciousness. And this opaqueness is apprehended as *indistinctness*. Indistinctness, which
under different forms is frequently utilized in
philosophy, is interiority seen from the outside;
or, if one prefers, indistinctness is the degraded
projection of interiority. This is the indistinctness, for example, that one may find in the famous "interpenetrative multiplicity" of Bergson.
It is also this indistinctness, anterior to the spec-
ifications of *natura naturata*, which one finds in
the God of many mystics. Now it may be interpreted as a primitive undifferentiation of all
qualities, now as a pure form of being, anterior
to all qualification. These two forms of indistinctness belong to the ego, according to our way of
considering it. In expectation, for example (or
when Marcel Arland explains that an extraordi-
nary event is necessary to reveal the true *me*),
the ego gives itself as a naked power which will
specify itself and congeal itself in contact with
events.[32] After action, on the contrary, it seems

that the ego reabsorbs the accomplished act into an interpenetrative multiplicity. In both cases, it is always a matter of a concrete totality, but the totalizing synthesis is effected by different intentions. Perhaps one could go so far as to say that the ego, with respect to the past, is interpenetrative multiplicity, and with respect to the future, bare power. But we should beware here of over-schematizing.

The *me*, as such, remains unknown to us. And this is easily understood. The *me* is given as an object. Therefore, the only method for knowing it is observation, approximation, anticipation, experience. But these procedures, which may be perfectly suited to any *non-intimate* transcendent, are not suitable here, because of the very intimacy of the *me*. It is too much present for one to succeed in taking a truly external viewpoint on it. If we step back for vantage, the *me* accompanies us in this withdrawal. It is infinitely near, and I cannot circle around it. Am I an idler or a hard worker? I shall doubtless come to a decision if I consult those who know me and get their opinion. Or, again, I can collect facts concerning myself and try to interpret them *as objectively as if it were a question about someone else*. But it would be useless to address myself directly to the *me*, and to try to benefit from its intimacy in order to know it. For it is the *me*, on the contrary, which bars our way. Thus, "really to know oneself" is inevitably to take toward oneself the point of view of others, that is to say, a point of view which is necessarily false. And all those who have tried to know themselves will admit that this introspective attempt shows itself from the start as an effort to reconstitute from detached pieces, from isolated fragments, what is originally given *all at once*, at a stroke. Also, the intuition of the ego is a constantly gulling mirage, for it simultaneously yields everything and yields nothing. How could it be otherwise, moreover, since the ego is not the real totality of consciousnesses (such a totality would be a contradiction, like any infinite unity enacted), but the *ideal* unity of all the states and actions? Being ideal, naturally, this unity can embrace an infinity of states. But one can well understand that what is given to the concrete, full intuition is only this unity *insofar* as it incorporates the present state. By virtue of this concrete nucleus a more or less sizeable quantity of empty intentions (by right, an infinity of them) are directed toward the past and toward the future, and aim at the states and actions not presently given. Those who have some acquaintance with Phenomenology will understand without difficulty that the ego may be at the same time an ideal unity of states, the majority of which are absent, and a concrete totality wholly giving itself to intuition: this signifies merely that the ego is a noematic rather than a noetic unity.[33] A tree or a chair exist no differently. Naturally, the empty intentions can always be fulfilled, and any state or action whatsoever can always reappear to consciousness as produced or having been produced by the ego.

Finally, what radically prevents the acquisition of real cognitions of the ego is the very special way in which it is given to reflective consciousness. The ego never appears, in fact, except when one is not looking at it. The reflective gaze must be fixed on the *Erlebnis*, insofar as it emanates from the state. Then, behind the state, at the horizon, the ego appears. It is, therefore, never seen except "out of the corner of the eye." As soon as I turn my gaze toward it and try to reach it without passing through the *Erlebnis* and the state, it vanishes. This is because in trying to apprehend the ego for itself and as a direct object of my consciousness, I fall back onto the unreflected level, and the ego disappears along with the reflective act. Whence that vexing sense of uncertainty, which many philosophers express by putting the *I* on this side of the state of consciousness and affirming that consciousness must return upon itself in order to perceive the *I* which is behind it. That is not it: rather, the ego is *by nature* fugitive.

It is certain, however, that the *I* does appear on the unreflected level. If someone asks me "What are you doing?" and I reply, all preoccupied, "I am trying to hang this picture," or "I am repairing the rear tire," these statements do not transport us to the level of reflection. I utter them without ceasing to work, without ceasing to envisage actions only as done or to be done—not insofar as I am doing them. But this "I" which is here in question nevertheless is no mere syntactical form. It has a meaning; it is quite simply an empty concept which is destined to remain empty. Just as I can think of a chair in the absence of any chair merely by a concept, I can in the same way think of the *I* in the absence of the *I*. This is what a consideration of states such as "What are you doing this afternoon?" "I am going to the office," or "I have met my friend Peter," or "I must write him," etc., makes obvious.

But the *I*, by falling from the reflective level to the unreflected level, does not simply empty itself. It degrades itself: it loses its *intimacy*. The concept could never be filled by the data of intuition, for now it aims at something other than those data. The *I* that we find here is in some way the support of actions that "I" do, or have to do, in the world insofar as these actions are qualities of the world and not unities of consciousnesses. For example, the wood *has to* be broken into small pieces for the fire to catch. It *has to:* this is a quality of the wood and an objective relation of the wood to the fire which *has to* be lighted. Now *I* am breaking the wood, that is to say, the action is realized in the world, and the objective and empty support of this action is the *I-concept*. This is why the body and bodily images can consummate the total degradation of the concrete *I* of reflection to the "*I*-concept" by functioning for the "*I*-concept" as its illusory fulfillment. I say: " 'I' break the wood and I see and feel the object, 'body,' engaged in breaking the wood." The body there serves as a visible and tangible symbol for the *I*. We see, then, the series of refractions and degradations with which an "egology" would be concerned:

Reflective level
$$\left\{\begin{array}{l}\text{Reflected consciousness: imma-}\\ \quad\text{nence, interiority.}\\ \text{Intuited ego: transcendence, in-}\\ \quad\text{timacy (the domain of the}\\ \quad\text{psychical).}\end{array}\right.$$

Unreflected level
$$\left\{\begin{array}{l}\textit{I}\text{-concept (optional): a tran-}\\ \quad\text{scendent which is empty,}\\ \quad\text{without "intimacy."}\\ \text{Body as the illusory fulfillment}\\ \quad\text{of the }\textit{I}\text{-concept (the domain}\\ \quad\text{of the psycho-physical).}\end{array}\right.$$

E. THE *I* AND CONSCIOUSNESS IN THE *cogito*

One might ask why the *I* appears on the occasion of the *Cogito*, since the *Cogito*, correctly performed, is an apprehension of a pure consciousness, without any constitution of states or actions. To tell the truth, the *I* is not necessary here, since it is never a direct unity of consciousnesses. One can even suppose a consciousness performing a pure reflective act which delivers consciousness to itself as a non-personal spontaneity. Only we must realize that phenomenological reduction is never perfect. Here intervene a host of psychological motivations. When Descartes performs the *Cogito*, he performs it in conjunction with methodological doubt, with the ambition of "advancing science," etc., which are *actions* and *states*. Thus the Cartesian method, doubt, etc., are by nature given as undertakings of an *I*. It is quite natural that the *Cogito*, which appears at the end of these undertakings, and *which is given as logically bound to methodological doubt*, sees an *I* appear on its horizon. This *I* is a form of ideal connection, a way of affirming that the *Cogito* is indeed of the same form as doubt. In a word, the *Cogito* is impure. It is a spontaneous consciousness, no doubt, but it remains synthetically tied to consciousnesses of states and actions. The proof is that the *Cogito* is given at once as the logical result of doubt and as that which puts an end to doubt. A reflective apprehension of spontaneous consciousness as non-personal spontaneity would have to be accomplished *without any antecedent motivation*. This is always possible in principle, but remains very improbable or, at least, extremely rare in our human condition. At any rate, as we have said above, the *I* which appears on the horizon of the *I Think* is not given as the producer of conscious spontaneity. Consciousness produces itself facing the *I* and goes toward it, goes to rejoin it. That is all one can say.

conclusions

In conclusion, we would like simply to offer the three following remarks:

1. The conception of the ego which we propose seems to us to effect the liberation of the Transcendental Field, and at the same time its purification.

The Transcendental Field, purified of all ego-logical structure, recovers its primary transparency. In a sense, it is a *nothing*, since all physical, psycho-physical, and psychic objects, all truths, all values are outside it; since my *me* has itself ceased to be any part of it. But this nothing is *all* since it is *consciousness of* all these objects. There is no longer an "inner life" in the sense in which Brunschvicg opposes "inner life" and "spiritual life," because there is no longer anything which is an *object* and which can at the same time partake of the intimacy of consciousness. Doubts, remorse, the so-called "mental crises of consciousness," etc.—in short, all the content of intimate diaries—become sheer *performance*. And perhaps we could derive here some sound precepts of moral discretion. But, in addition, we must bear in mind that from this point of view my emotions and my states, my ego itself, cease to be my exclusive property. To be precise: up to now a radical distinction has been made between the objectivity of a spatio-temporal thing or of an external truth, and the subjectivity of psychical "states." It seemed as if the subject had a privileged status with respect to his own states. When two men, according to this conception, talk about the same chair, they really are talking about the *same* thing. This chair which one takes hold of and lifts is *the same* as the chair which the other sees. There is not merely a correspondence of images; there is only one object. But it seemed that when Paul tried to understand a psychical state of Peter, he could not *reach* this state, the intuitive apprehension of which belonged only to Peter. He could only envisage an equivalent, could only create empty concepts which tried in vain to reach a reality by essence removed from intuition. Psychological

understanding occurred by analogy. Phenomenology has come to teach us that *states* are objects, that an emotion as such (a love or a hatred)
is a transcendent object and cannot shrink into
the interior unity of a "consciousness." Consequently, if Paul and Peter both speak of Peter's
love, for example, it is no longer true that the
one speaks blindly and by analogy of that which
the other apprehends in full. They speak of the
same thing. Doubtless they apprehend it by different procedures, but these procedures may be
equally intuitional.[34] And Peter's emotion is no
more *certain* for Peter than for Paul. For both of
them, it belongs to the category of objects which
can be called into question. But the whole of this
profound and novel conception is compromised
if the *me* of Peter, that *me* which hates or which
loves, remains an essential structure of consciousness. The emotion, after all, remains at-
tached to the *me*. This emotion "sticks to" the
me. If one draws the *me* into consciousness, one
draws the emotion along with it. To us, it
seemed, on the contrary, that the *me* was a transcendent object, like the *state*, and that because
of this fact it was accessible to two sorts of intuition: an intuitive apprehension by the consciousness *of which it is the me*, and an intuitive appre-

hension less clear, but no less intuitive, by other consciousnesses. In a word, Peter's *me* is accessible to my intuition as well as to Peter's intuition, and in both cases it is the object of inadequate evidence. If that is the case, then there is no longer anything "impenetrable" about Peter; unless it is his very consciousness. But his consciousness is *radically* impenetrable. We mean that it is not only refractory to intuition, but to thought.[35] I cannot *conceive* Peter's consciousness without making an object of it (since I do not conceive it as being *my consciousness*). I cannot conceive it because I would have to think of it as pure interiority and as transcendence *at the same time*, which is impossible. A consciousness cannot conceive of a consciousness other than itself. Thus we can distinguish, thanks to our conception of the *me*, a sphere accessible to psychology, in which the method of external observation and the introspective method have the same rights and can mutually assist each other, and a pure transcendental sphere accessible to phenomenology alone.

This transcendental sphere is a sphere of *absolute* existence, that is to say, a sphere of pure spontaneities which are never objects and which determine their own existence. The *me* being an object, it is evident that I shall never be able to say: *my* consciousness, that is, the consciousness of my *me* (save in a purely designative sense, as one says for example: the day *of my* baptism). The ego is not the owner of consciousness; it is the object of consciousness. To be sure, we constitute spontaneously our states and actions as productions of the ego. But our states and actions are also objects. We never have a direct intuition of the spontaneity of an instantaneous consciousness as produced by the ego. That would be impossible. It is only on the level of meanings and psychological hypotheses that we can conceive such production—and this error is possible only because on this level the ego and the consciousness are indicated *emptily*.[36] In this sense, if one understands the *I Think* so as to make of thought a production of the *I*, one has already constituted thought as passivity and as *state*, that is to say, as object. One has left the level of pure reflection, in which the ego undoubtedly appears, but appears *on the horizon* of a spontaneity. The reflective attitude is correctly expressed in this famous sentence by Rimbaud (in the letter of the seer): "I is *an other*." The context proves that he simply meant that the spontaneity of consciousness could not emanate from the *I*, the spontaneity *goes toward* the *I*, rejoins the *I*, lets the *I* be glimpsed beneath its limpid density, but is itself given above all as *individuated* and *impersonal* spontaneity. The commonly accepted thesis, according to which our thoughts would gush from an impersonal unconscious and would "personalize" themselves by becoming conscious, seems to us a coarse and materialistic interpretation of a correct intuition. It has been maintained by psychologists who have very well understood that consciousness does not "come out" of the *I*, but who could not accept the idea of a spontaneity producing itself. These psychologists therefore naively imagined that the spontaneous consciousnesses "came out" of the unconscious where they already existed, without realizing that they had only put off the problem of existence, which really had to be formulated in the end, and which they had obscured, since the antecedent existence of spontaneities within preconscious limits would necessarily be *passive* existence.

We may therefore formulate our thesis: transcendental consciousness is an impersonal spontaneity. It determines its existence at each instant, without our being able to conceive anything *before* it. Thus each instant of our conscious life reveals to us a creation *ex nihilo*. Not a new *arrangement*, but a new existence. There is something distressing for each of us, to catch in the act this tireless creation of existence of which *we* are not the creators. At this level man has the impression of ceaselessly escaping from himself, of overflowing himself, of being surprised by riches which are always unexpected. And once more it is an unconscious from which he demands an account of this surpassing of the *me* by consciousness. Indeed, the *me* can do nothing to this spontaneity, for *will is an object which constitutes itself for and by this spontaneity*. The will directs itself upon states, upon emotions, or upon things, but it never turns back upon consciousness. We are well aware of this in the occasional cases in which we try *to will* a consciousness (I *will* fall asleep, I *will* no longer think about that, etc.). In these various cases, it is *by essence* necessary that the will be maintained and preserved *by that consciousness which is radically opposed* to the consciousness it wants to give rise to (if I *will* to fall asleep, I stay awake; if I *will* not to think about this or that, I think about it *precisely on that account*). It seems to us that this monstrous spontaneity is at the origin of numerous psychasthenic ailments.

Consciousness is frightened by its own spontaneity because it senses this spontaneity as *beyond*
freedom. This is clearly seen in an example from
Janet. A young bride was in terror, when her
husband left her alone, of sitting at the window
and summoning the passers-by like a prostitute.
Nothing in her education, in her past, nor in her
character could serve as an explanation of such a
fear. It seems to us simply that a negligible cir-
cumstance (reading, conversation, etc.) had determined in her what one might call "a vertigo of
possibility." She found herself monstrously free,
and this vertiginous freedom appeared to her *at
the opportunity* for this action which she was
afraid of doing. But this vertigo is comprehensi-
ble only if consciousness suddenly appeared to
itself as infinitely overflowing in its possibilities
the *I* which ordinarily serves as its unity.

Perhaps, in reality, the essential function of the
ego is not so much theoretical as practical. We
have noticed, indeed, that it does not bind up the
unity of phenomena; that it is limited to reflecting an *ideal* unity, whereas the real and concrete
unity has long been effected. But perhaps the essential role of the ego is to mask from consciousness its very spontaneity. A phenomenological
description of spontaneity would show, indeed,

that spontaneity renders impossible any distinction between action and passion, or any conception of an autonomy of the will. These notions have meaning only on a level where all activity is given as emanating from a passivity which it transcends; in short, on a level at which man considers himself as at once subject and object. But it is an essential necessity that one not be able to distinguish between voluntary spontaneity and involuntary spontaneity.

Everything happens, therefore, as if consciousness constituted the ego as a false representation of itself, as if consciousness hypnotized itself before this ego which it has constituted, absorbing itself in the ego as if to make the ego its guardian and its law. It is thanks to the ego, indeed, that a distinction can be made between the possible and the real, between appearance and being, between the willed and the undergone.

But it can happen that consciousness suddenly produces itself on the pure reflective level. Perhaps not without the ego, yet as escaping from the ego on all sides, as dominating the ego and maintaining the ego outside the consciousness by a continued creation. On this level, there is no distinction between the possible and the real, since the appearance is the absolute. There are no more barriers, no more limits, nothing to hide consciousness from itself. Then consciousness, noting what could be called the fatality of its spontaneity, is suddenly anguished: it is this dread, absolute and without remedy, this fear of itself, which seems to us constitutive of pure consciousness, and which holds the key to the psychasthenic ailment we spoke of. If the *I* of the *I Think* is the primary structure of consciousness, this dread is impossible. If, on the contrary, our point of view is adopted, not only do we have a coherent explanation of this ailment, but we have, moreover, a permanent motive for carrying out the phenomenological reduction. As we know, in his article in *Kantstudien*[37] Fink admits, not without some melancholy, that as long as one remains in the "natural" attitude, there is *no reason*, no "motive" for exercising the ἐποχή. In fact, this natural attitude is perfectly coherent. There one will find none of those contradictions which, according to Plato, lead the philosopher to effect a philosophical conversion. Thus, the ἐποχή appears in the phenomenology of Husserl as a miracle. Husserl himself, in *Cartesianische Meditationen*,[38] made an extremely vague allusion to certain psychological motives which would lead to undertaking reduction. But these motives hardly seem sufficient. Moreover, reduction seems capable of being performed only at the end of lengthy study. It appears, then, as a *knowledgeable* operation, which confers on it a sort of gratuitousness. On the other hand, if "the natural attitude" appears wholly as an effort made by consciousness to escape from itself by projecting itself into the *me* and becoming absorbed there, and if this effort is never completely rewarded, and if a simple act of reflection suffices in order for conscious spontaneity to tear itself abruptly away from the *I* and be given as independent, then the ἐποχή is no longer a miracle, an intellectual method, an erudite procedure: it is an anxiety which is imposed on us and which we cannot avoid: it is both a pure event of transcendental origin and an ever possible accident of our daily life.

2. This conception of the ego seems to us the only possible refutation of solipsism. The refutation that Husserl presents in *Formale und Transzendentale Logik*[39] and in *Cartesianische Meditationen*[40] does not seem to us capable of unsettling a determined and intelligent solipsist. As long as the *I* remains a structure of consciousness, it will always remain possible to oppose consciousness, with its *I*, to all other existents.

Finally, then, it is really the *me* who must pro-duce the world. Small matter if certain layers of this world necessitate by their very nature a rela-tion to others. This relation can be a mere quality of the world that I create and in no way obliges me to accept the real existence of other *I*'s.

But if the *I* becomes a transcendent, it partici-pates in all the vicissitudes of the world. It is no absolute; it has not created the universe; it falls like other existences at the stroke of the ἐποχή; and solipsism becomes unthinkable from the moment that the *I* no longer has a privileged sta-tus. Instead of expressing itself in effect as "I alone exist as absolute," it must assert that "ab-solute consciousness alone exists as absolute," which is obviously a truism. My *I*, in effect, is *no more certain for consciousness than the I of other men*. It is only more intimate.

3. The theorists of the extreme Left have some-times reproached phenomenology for being an idealism and for drowning reality in the stream of ideas. But if idealism is the philosophy with-out evil of Brunschvicg, if it is a philosophy in which the effort of spiritual assimilation never meets external resistances, in which suffering, hunger, and war are diluted in a slow process of the unification of ideas, nothing is more unjust

than to call phenomenologists "idealists." On the contrary, for centuries we have not felt in philosophy so realistic a current. The phenomenologists have plunged man back into the world; they have given full measure to man's agonies and sufferings, and also to his rebellions. Unfortunately, as long as the *I* remains a structure of absolute consciousness, one will still be able to reproach phenomenology for being an escapist doctrine, for again pulling a part of man out of the world and, in that way, turning our attention from the real problems. It seems to us that this reproach no longer has any justification if one makes the *me* an existent, strictly contemporaneous with the world, whose existence has the same essential characteristics as the world. It has always seemed to me that a working hypothesis as fruitful as historical materialism never needed for a foundation the absurdity which is metaphysical materialism. In fact, it is not necessary that the object precede the subject for spiritual pseudo-values to vanish and for ethics to find its bases in reality. It is enough that the *me* be contemporaneous with the World, and that the subject-object duality, which is purely logical, definitively disappear from philosophical preoccupations. The World has not created the *me*;

the *me* has not created the World. These are two objects for absolute, impersonal consciousness, and it is by virtue of this consciousness that they are connected. This absolute consciousness, when it is purified of the *I*, no longer has anything of the *subject*. It is no longer a collection of representations. It is quite simply a first condition and an absolute source of existence. And the relation of interdependence established by this absolute consciousness between the *me* and the World is sufficient for the *me* to appear as "endangered" before the World, for the *me* (indirectly and through the intermediary of states) to draw the whole of its content from the World. No more is needed in the way of a philosophical foundation for an ethics and a politics which are absolutely positive.

notes

1. I shall use here the term "consciousness" ["*conscience*"] to translate the German word *Bewusstsein*, which signifies both the whole of consciousness—the monad—and each moment of this consciousness. The expression "state of consciousness" seems to me inaccurate owing to the passivity which it introduces into consciousness. [AUTHOR.]

2. No single term is more central to phenomenology and more alien to current trends in British and American philosophy than the term "intui-

tion." Its exposition would merit an essay longer than this translation. The interested reader is referred to the classic discussions by Edmund Husserl in "Ideen Zur Einer Reinen Phänomenologie Und Phänomenologischen Philosophie —Volume I," published in *Jahrbuch Für Philosophie Und Phänomenologische Forschung*, I (1922), pp. 1-323 (henceforth abbreviated *Ideen I*). An English translation to which the reader may refer by Section numbers is published under the title *Ideas* (New York: Macmillan, 1931). The most relevant passages are in Secs. 1-4, 7, and 18-24.

Perhaps the essential point to be retained in connection with this phenomenologically oriented essay by Sartre is that for the phenomenologist the primary mode of evidence is intuitive. An intuition (summarily explained) is an act of consciousness by which the object under investigation is *confronted*, rather than merely indicated *in absentia*. Thus, it is one thing merely to indicate the Eiffel Tower (merely "to have it in mind," as we say), and another thing to confront the indicated object by an act of imagination or perception. The indicative act is "empty"; the intuitive act of imagination or perception is "filled out." Once this distinction has been made, it would seem difficult to disagree with the phenomenologist that every cognitive inquiry must ultimately base its claims upon acts of intuition, even if supplementary modes of evidence (e.g., inductive reasoning regarding the external world which is confronted by perceptual intuition) must be invoked to develop the inquiry. For an object must be present, confronted, to be investigated, however far from such original confrontation the investigation may wander as it proceeds. In the physical sciences, the reliance in the last analysis upon perceptual evidence is patent. In phenomenology, the subject matter under investigation is consciousness. The method is intuitive, then, in the sense that consciousness must regard itself to determine just what consciousness is, what consciousness does and does not include. In the present essay, of course, the issue is whether consciousness is or is not inhabited by an "I" or ego operating within or behind consciousness. When Sartre writes in the present passage, therefore, that phenomenology is a "scientific" rather than a "Critical" study of consciousness because phenomenology proceeds by "intuition," he means that as in any descriptive science the first requirement is to *look at* the subject matter, in contrast to Kantian philosophy, which might be said to begin with the nature of science and to construct subsequently an account of consciousness by inference.

Owing to the impracticality of a detailed account in this place of the phenomenological concept of intuition, it may be helpful to note briefly some familiar senses of "intuition" which would be quite out of place. First, intuitive knowledge has no traffic with mystical insight. The "filling out" of a previously empty consciousness of an object represents a logically distinct kind of consciousness, not some flow of feeling. Second, intuitive knowledge is not an identification with the object in the Bergsonian sense. Third, intuitive knowledge is not limited to the familiar type of intuition of the external world which we call "sense-perception." Intuition may be directed to consciousness itself (i. e., introspectively). Intuition may be directed to a highly complex object, i. e., a "state of affairs," previously set forth for consciousness by a process of judgment. For example, I may confront by an act of intuition the state of affairs "that this knife is to the right of the plate." Fourth, as may be evident from the last example, intuition is possible at any level of abstraction (e.g., I may confront in intuition the genus Red). Fifth, almost invariably to intuit an object or state of affairs is not to know its existence (e.g., to imagine the Eiffel Tower and to perceive the Eiffel Tower are both intuitive confrontations of the object). The exception concerns reflective intuition of the specious present. Sixth, to intuit an object is not necessarily to know everything about it, viz., the inadequacy of sense-perception, which is always an apprehension of the object "in profile." (Cf. below, n. 17, on the alleged inadequacy of intuition of the ego.) Thus, the notion of intuition in phenomenology does not necessarily imply the notion of certain knowledge. Yet the primary mode of evidence in any cognitive inquiry must be intuitive, according to the phenomenologist, for to learn, one must at the very least confront some of the objects in question, e.g., physical things, psychological states, number, principles of logic. [TRS.]

3. Husserl would say, "a science of essences." But, for the point of view we adopt, it amounts to the same. [AUTHOR.] In a study of consciousness by consciousness, *what* present consciousness is (its essence) and *that* it is (the fact that it exists) obviously make up only one question. Consequently, Sartre speaks indifferently of an "essential" and a "factual" inquiry. This would not appear to be orthodox Husserlian phenomenology (viz., *Ideen I*, Introduction). [TRS.]

4. The *epoché* (ἐποχή) is an act of withdrawal from the usual assertiveness of consciousness regarding what does and does not exist in the world. The effect of this withdrawal is to re-

veal the world as a correlate of consciousness. The term "reduction" employed in the same paragraph has the same meaning. (Cf. *Ideen I*, Secs. 31-34.) [TRS.]

5. Halle, 1900-1901 (5th Investigation, Sec. 4). See also, Marvin Farber, *The Foundation of Phenomenology* (Cambridge, 1943), pp. 337-338. [TRS.]

6. Cf. *Ideen I*, Sec. 57. [TRS.]

7. Two paragraphs below Sartre asserts that "consciousness is defined by intentionality." Five paragraphs after that assertion, reference is made once more to "the fruitful definition cited earlier." Strictly speaking, Husserl never concerned himself with a final definition, but certainly he regarded intentionality as essential to consciousness, i.e., consciousness is necessarily consciousness *of something*. (Cf. *Ideen I*, Sec. 84.) [TRS.]

8. Published in *Jahrbuch für Philosophie und Phänomenologische Forschung*, IX (1928), pp. 367-498. [TRS.]

9. Published in *Husserliana*, I (1950), pp. 1-183. A French translation by G. Peiffer & E. Levinas is published under the title *Méditations Cartésiennes* (Paris, J. Vrin, 1947). For the discussion of temporal unifications, see esp. Secs. 18 & 37. [TRS.]

10. Cf. *op. cit.*, "Meditation V." [TRS.]

11. The phrase is quoted from *Ideen I*, Sec. 46. In the *Cogito*, the fact that the *Cogito* is taking place is necessarily so. [TRS.]

12. Cf. *op. cit.* [TRS.]

13. Cf. *Ideen I*, Sec. 84. [TRS.]

14. Cf. E. B Titchener, *Textbook of Psychology* (New York: Macmillan, 1919), pp. 544-545. [TRS.]

15. Cf. above, Part I, Sec. A. [TRS.]

16. The awkwardness alluded to is presumably the attempt made by Husserl in Section 61 of *Ideen I* to distinguish essences into two types, "transcendent" and "immanent." A consciousness not inhabited by an ego would doubtless have no "immanent essences," thus obviating the necessity for such a distinction. [TRS.]

17. The "I" is grasped "with evidence" in reflection in the sense that the "I" is intuitively apprehended (cf. above, n. 2). Evidence is "adequate" when the object in question is grasped in its entirety (e.g., perceptual intuition is always inadequate evidence). Evidence is "apodictic" when the object or state of affairs in question is apprehended as being necessarily thus-and-so (e.g., that color is extended may be known apodictically). Sartre points out that the "I" with which reflective intuition is confronted is grasped neither adequately nor apodictically [TRS.]

18. Cf. Eugen Fink, "Die Phänomenologische Philosophie Edmund Husserls In Der Gegenwartigen Kritik. Mit Einem Vorwort Von Edmund Husserl," *Kantstudien*, XXXVIII (1933), pp. 356 ff., 381ff. [TRS.]

19. It will be recalled (see above, n. 2 and n. 17) that there are no mystical or magical connotations to this "special kind" of "intuition." In reflection, consciousness can intuit the "I" in a "special" manner in the sense that confronting this transcendent object is not the same as, say, confronting a physical thing by an act of perceptual intuition. [TRS.]

20. The term "noematic correlate" (or "noema") is employed in phenomenology to refer to the terminus of an intention as given for consciousness (e. g., this book as the object of consciousness). The noematic correlate does not necessarily exist in fact. The "noesis" is the apprehension which is directed upon the noema. (Cf. *Ideen I*, Secs. 85 *et seq.*) [TRS.]

21. Cf. *Vorlesungen Zur Phänomenologie des Inneren Zeitbewusstseins, op. cit., passim.* [AUTHOR.]

22. Regarding the term "noematic" here and elsewhere, cf. n. 20, above. [TRS.]

23. The French text contains the phrase *sans l'influence*, which we have read as a misprint for *sous l'influence*. [TRS].

24. But it can also be aimed at and reached through perception of behavior. We hope to explain in some other place the deep-seated identity of *all* psychological methods. [AUTHOR.]

25. *Ideen I*, Sec. 131, p. 270. [AUTHOR.]

26. We may add that Husserl was well acquainted with this type of synthetic totality, to which he devoted a remarkable study in *Logische Untersuchungen* [*op. cit.*], vol. II, pt. 1, Investigation No. 3. [AUTHOR.] Cf. Marvin Farber, *op cit.*, ch. X, pp. 283-312. [TRS.]

27. Halle, Niemeyer, 1929, vol. I, pp. 364-366, & *passim.* [TRS.]

28. Since the fundamental source of evidence is intuition (see above, n. 2), evidential experiences prior to explicit judgment are possible. [TRS.]

29. Cf. J.-P. Sartre, *L'Imaginaire. Psychologie Phénoménologique de l'Imagination* (Paris: Librairie Gallimard, 1940), pp. 201ff. Published in English under the title *The Psychology of Imagination* (New York: Philosophical Library, 1948). [TRS.]

30. Cf. Henri Bergson, *Time And Free Will*, tr. F. L. Pogosn, (New York: Macmillan, 1910), pp. 219-221. [TRS.]

31. The pun on "meurtrissure" is virtually untranslatable. It expresses with ingenuity the sense in which the murderous deed of Raskolnikov (*le*

meurtre) affects in kind his murderous ego in the form of a bruise to the ego (*une meurtrissure*). [TRS.]

32. As in the case of the overwrought man who, wanting to signify that he does not know how far his emotion will carry him, cries: "I am afraid of *myself*." [AUTHOR.]

33. The allusion is to the phenomenological principle remarked by Sartre in Part I, Sec. A, above, that objects are given to consciousness through "facets" (*Abschattungen*). Thus, an object is an *ideal* unity. On the other hand, in contrast to Kant, the phenomenologists generally hold that the object is not an unknowable thing-in-itself, for the ideal unity is indeed given *as such* to consciousness. (Regarding the terms "noematic" and "noetic," see above, n. 20.) [TRS.]

34. This is only to say that Peter and Paul may both directly confront by an act of consciousness the public object which is the ego of Peter. (Cf. above, n. 2, on "intuition.") [TRS.]

35. The difficulty regarding another consciousness, in other words, is not like the difficulty regarding the other side of the moon, which can be thought (but never intuited, because it so happens we always see the same face). From no *conceivable* vantage-point could we be confronted by another consciousness. [TRS.]

36. When we see the words "this book," in all

likelihood we will indicate this book emptily; we will "merely have it in mind." Were we to *imagine* this book, however, or actually *look at* the book, we would have "filled out" our consciousness of it; we would have confronted the object by an act of intuition. (Cf. above, n. 2.) The belief that the ego can produce consciousness remains possible only so long as one does not attempt to verify it intuitively, by "looking to see" if it is so. [TRS.]

37. Cf. Eugen Fink, *loc. cit.*, pp. 346-351. [TRS.]

38. Cf. *op. cit.*, Sec. 1. [TRS.]

39. Halle, Niemeyer, 1929, pp. 205-215. [TRS.]

40. Cf. *op. cit.*, "Meditation V." [TRS.]